Our Lady of the Angels

A Celebration in Color and Light

Written by Rev. Leo Larrivee, S.S. ✠ Photography by Jim Stratton

Special thanks to Fr. John Bowen, S.S., Archivist Emeritus, Society of St. Sulpice.

ISBN 10: 1-59152-051-7
ISBN 13: 978-1-59152-051-1

© 2009 Our Lady of the Angels Chapel
Photography © 2009 by Jim Stratton

Produced by Sweetgrass Books, a division of Farcountry Press, Helena, MT 59601, (800) 821-3874
Printed in China.

12 11 10 09   1 2 3 4 5 6

The story of Our Lady of the Angels Chapel begins in 1848 with the opening of St. Charles College in Ellicott City, Maryland. St. Charles College was the first Catholic minor seminary in the United States. The cornerstone for the school had been laid in 1831, and the land on which the college was built was donated by Charles Carroll of Carrollton, the only Catholic to have signed the Declaration of Independence, and the last of the signers to die. Carroll donated the land at the request of Archbishop Ambrose Marechal, third Archbishop of Baltimore, who was a Sulpician and former president of St. Mary's Seminary.

At first Carroll was reluctant to make the donation but was convinced by his favorite granddaughter, Emily Caton MacTavish, who lived with her family in what would become Catonsville, Maryland. Carroll witnessed the laying of the cornerstone but did not live to see the opening of the college. The college was named for St. Charles Borromeo, the bishop of Milan, Italy, who was very influential in the beginning of the seminary movement for the formation of priests in Italy, and who was also Charles Carroll's patron saint. The college was founded by the Sulpician Fathers, who had come to this country from France in 1791 as refugees of the French Revolution. Founded by Jean Jacques Olier in 1641 at St. Sulpice Church in Paris, the Sulpicians' primary mission has been and continues to be the academic and spiritual formation of future priests. They had been invited to this country by Bishop John Carroll of Baltimore and, led by Fr. Francois Nagot, they founded St. Mary's Seminary in Baltimore in 1791.

FACING PAGE: *Original St. Charles College, Ellicott City, Maryland (courtesy of the Sulpician Archives)*

TOP, RIGHT: *Charles Carroll*

BOTTOM, RIGHT: *St. Charles Borromeo*

The first president of St. Charles College was a Sulpician priest, Fr. Oliver Jenkins, S.S. The original chapel of **Our Lady of the Angels** was begun in 1860 on the Ellicott City site, but was not finished until 1866 because of interruptions caused by the Civil War. The chapel was designed by a Sulpician priest, Fr. Faillon, a trained architect and friend of Fr. Jenkins who was in the country as representative of the Sulpician superior in Paris. Fr. Faillon modeled the chapel after the Sainte Chapelle in Paris, which had been built by King Louis IX and was completed in the year 1248. Sainte Chapelle was close to St. Sulpice in Paris, and Fr. Faillon would have been familiar with its design. The chapel was built with funds donated by Fr. Jenkins and members of his family, and it was dedicated on July 11, 1866, by Archbishop Martin Spalding, the sixth Archbishop of Baltimore. While the construction of the chapel structure was completed relatively quickly, the interior of the chapel took many years to finish. A beautiful white marble altar was gifted by a granddaughter of Charles Carroll, Miss Emily Harper. Above the altar was a life-size statue of Mary. The interior was richly decorated with murals, statues, and stained-glass windows, which were gifts of members of the Jenkins family. Not until 1886 was the Steere and Turner pipe organ installed and the major work completed. Unfortunately Fr. Jenkins did not live to see the completion of the chapel. He died in 1869 and was buried in the Sulpician cemetery on the grounds of the college and remained there until the graves were moved to the new Sulpician cemetery in Catonsville in 1929. The faculty and seminarians worshipped in this **Our Lady of the Angels Chapel** for close to fifty years.

FACING PAGE: *Original Our Lady of the Angels Chapel, Ellicott City, Maryland (courtesy of the Sulpician Archives)*

TOP, RIGHT: *Father Jenkins—first president of St. Charles College*

BOTTOM, RIGHT: *Father Nagot—founder of St. Mary's Seminary*

On March 16, 1911, Our Lady of the Angels Chapel—along with the rest of the college—burned to the ground. The fire started in the boiler room directly below the chapel, but the cause of the blaze was never discovered. Only six weeks earlier two windows of a new series ordered for the chapel from England had been installed. The new chapel windows were to be the finishing touch of a grand renovation planned for the college in 1898—the year of its golden jubilee. Thankfully no one was hurt in the fire, but the college and its beautiful chapel were destroyed. The ruins of the college can be seen to this day at Terra Maria in Ellicott City.

The ruins of St. Charles College, Ellicott City, Maryland

At the suggestion of Cardinal James Gibbons, the ninth Archbishop of Baltimore, who had attended St. Charles from 1855–1857, the college was moved to Cloud Cap, a farm in Catonsville, Maryland, owned by the Sulpicians. The land had been purchased by them in 1885 as a summer retreat. The Cloud Cap property had a long and interesting history, and again there was a connection to the Carroll family, as it was originally part of the vast land holdings of Charles Carroll. In 1822 he gave control of the property to his son-in-law Richard Caton, who lived nearby with his wife, Mary, and their daughters. The part of the estate that would come to be known as Cloud Cap was eventually given to Carroll's favorite granddaughter, Emily Caton, Richard and Mary's daughter, who would later marry John MacTavish. Later, in 1830, Emily Caton would persuade her grandfather to donate the land for St. Charles in Ellicott City. The Cloud Cap land was sold, and the Sulpicians eventually acquired it from Dr. Nathan Smith. It was here that the new St. Charles opened—only eleven days after the fire—in the original farmhouse, later called the Frederick House. It was named after Fr. Frederick, who had purchased it for the seminary, along with a building that later served as the college science building. Both buildings are still in use today, the latter housing the Development Group of Erickson Retirement Communities. The first chapel was a room in the farmhouse. Some temporary buildings, referred to as "the shacks," were also quickly built so the faculty could at least finish the 1911 school year and then make a decision about the future of the college. These few buildings, and two others on the other side of Maidenchoice Lane, became a temporary home to more than 200 faculty members and students.

Cardinal James Gibbons

Senior Dormitory.

Administration Building.

Junior

When the faculty of St. Mary's Seminary said they would give the Cloud Cap property to the college, the decision was made not to rebuild in Ellicott City but to remain in Catonsville. The Ellicott City property reverted to the heirs of Charles Carroll as stipulated in his will, and plans were envisioned for a new St. Charles College in Catonsville. All that remained in Ellicott City were the ruins of the seminary and the Sulpician cemetery, which would not be relocated until 1929.

The original plan for the new college was developed by Baltimore architect Charles Ulrich, who envisioned a very grand edifice with a main building and two wings, much like the building in Ellicott City. The chapel was planned for the center rear of the main building. This original plan was greatly scaled back, and only the main building and one wing were constructed for the housing and education of the seminarians. Construction began on March 14, 1912, but because of the lack of funds only one floor of the main building was completed, and it remained that way until 1929 when Archbishop Michael Curley, the tenth Archbishop of Baltimore, donated the funds for the completion of the building.

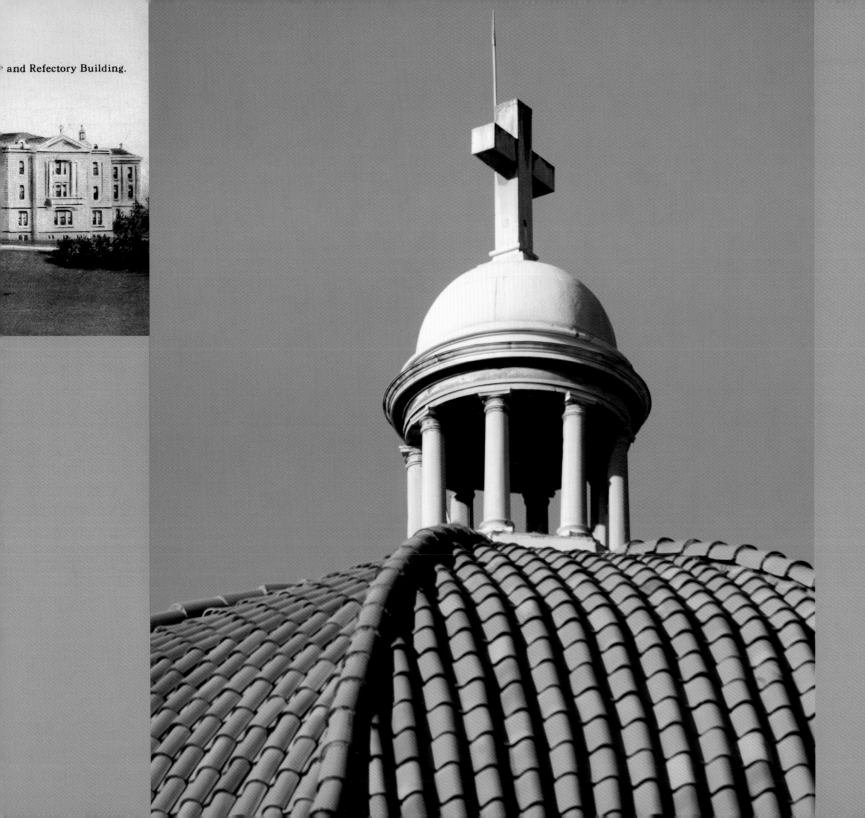

and Refectory Building.

15

Elizabeth Jenkins

Alfred Jenkins

The new chapel was not included in the original buildings, however, and its construction would have to wait until funds were available. For the time being, a trunk room in the basement had to suffice. Luckily donors would be found, and ground for the new **Our Lady of the Angels Chapel** was broken by Cardinal Gibbons on September 29, 1913. The cornerstone was laid by Cardinal Gibbons on St. Charles Day, November 4 of the same year. The plan envisioned a bell tower with the chapel in the Italian style, but the tower was never built. Romanesque in structure and Italian Renaissance in style, the chapel was built on the model of a basilica, in the shape of a cross with a main aisle crossed by two transepts as well as two side aisles,

all crowned with a dome and cupola. An ambulatory behind the marble altar as well as seven small chapels were also constructed. **Our Lady of the Angels Chapel** was designed by the firm of Murphy and Olmsted of Washington, D.C. Frederick Murphy had founded the Department of Architecture at Catholic University in 1911 and contributed greatly to the planning of that campus. Robert and Elizabeth Jenkins provided the funds for the construction of the chapel and established an endowment to care for it and complete the interior in memory of their parents, Alfred and Elizabeth Jenkins, who were members of an old and established Maryland family whose fortune had come from shipping, banking, and silversmithing.

A chalice commissioned by the Jenkinses from their family business was given to the chapel in 1916 in memory of their parents and is still in use today. Robert and Elizabeth were related to Fr. Oliver Jenkins, the first president of St. Charles in Ellicott City. The parents and children lie entombed beneath the marble floor in a memorial chapel to the side of the sanctuary. Robert and Elizabeth, who never married, traveled extensively in Europe, visiting many churches. They requested that various features from different churches be incorporated into the new chapel, and so **Our Lady of the Angels** Chapel copies no particular European church but rather contains features of various churches that appealed to the Jenkinses. At their suggestion the new chapel was built not as part of the main building but as a freestanding structure on the side of the main building where another dorm building had been planned but not built. Though the chapel was dedicated by Cardinal Gibbons in 1915, it was not fully completed for many years. The aforementioned reason for this was that the Jenkinses provided funds for the construction of the chapel and an endowment for the completion of the interior work.

The interior work on the chapel proceeded only when made possible by the income from the endowment. So the work took place in phases, and it was never really finished according to the Jenkins's original specifications, which, as requested in their will, would have included more mosaics on the ceiling of the nave. Over the years, however, this original shell was transformed into a magnificent space. In the Sulpician archives there is an interesting collection of letters between the Jenkinses and Rev. Edward Dyer, S.S., the Superior of the Sulpicians, concerning the interior of the new chapel. They all contributed ideas for the interior decoration of the chapel, although Fr. Dyer made the final decisions. The overall theme of the chapel decorations is the Priesthood of Jesus Christ.

Altar details

The marble altar, which is the centerpiece of the entire chapel, was sculpted by John J. Earley of Washington, D.C., who is also credited with inventing the concepts used in the fabrication of the altar. The core is precast aggregate concrete, which is covered with marble panels and then inlaid with intricate mosaics, semiprecious stones, and carved marble friezes. Six beautiful candlesticks adorn the altar along with many angels and statues. The mosaics on the back of the altar are especially fine examples of Italian Florentine marble mosaics. The Tree of Life in the center, representing the seven days of creation, is one of the finest works of art in the entire chapel. This mosaic is flanked by twin mosaics of grapes and wheat reminding one of the Eucharist. The small mosaics on the front of the altar are of Abraham about to sacrifice Isaac, and Melchisedeck, the High Priest who offered a sacrifice of bread and wine. These call attention to part of the prayer the priest would say at Mass, "accept this sacrifice as once you accepted the sacrifice of Abraham our father in the faith and the bread and wine offered by Your priest Melchisedeck."

The Tree of Life mosaic (behind the altar)

In the front of the base of the altar are the evangelists, Matthew, Mark, Luke, and John, who told the story of Jesus in their gospels. The theme of the upper section of the altar is the Transfiguration. Moses and Elijah are on either side of the glorified Jesus who is in the tabernacle. The crucifix, inlaid with lapis and precious stones, is above the tabernacle, with its silver door, rising into the blue-lined baldachino with the stars and the sun of heaven. This was to remind the seminarians that Jesus, as he said to his disciples, must rise to the glory of heaven through his death on the cross. On the top step in front of the altar are mosaics of palm trees fashioned from malachite and lapis.

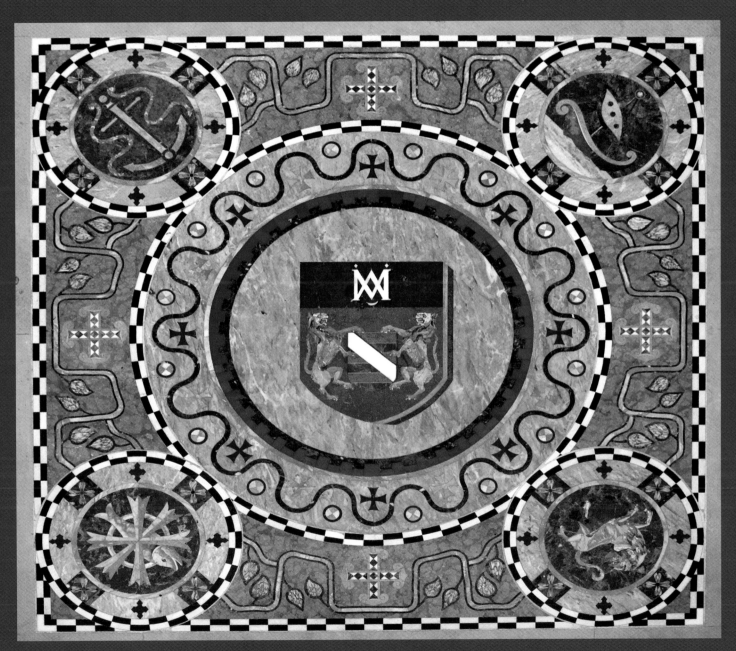

Center mosaic under the altar, combining the coat of arms of Charles Carroll with that of the Sulpician Fathers

The walls of the chapel are entirely lined with Cararra marble imported from Italy. The beautifully and naturally veined marble was quarried in blocks and sliced into panels. The panels were then numbered so that sections from the same block could be lined up on the walls so as to match perfectly. The effect is spectacular, and in this country only in the Library of Congress will one find a comparable interior. Space was left between the panels of marble, which was then filled with gold and tile mosaics in the early 1940s. All of the massive columns in the chapel are of

The first marble was shipped from Italy in 1917 but was sunk by a German submarine as World War I was still raging. Another entire supply of marble had to be quarried, and the marble in the chapel was not installed until 1920–1921. While the marble was being installed, worship services were held in the basement of the chapel. After the installation of the marble, the chapel was formally opened on St. Charles Day, November 4, 1922. Cardinal Gibbons had died in 1921, and the ceremony was presided over by Archbishop

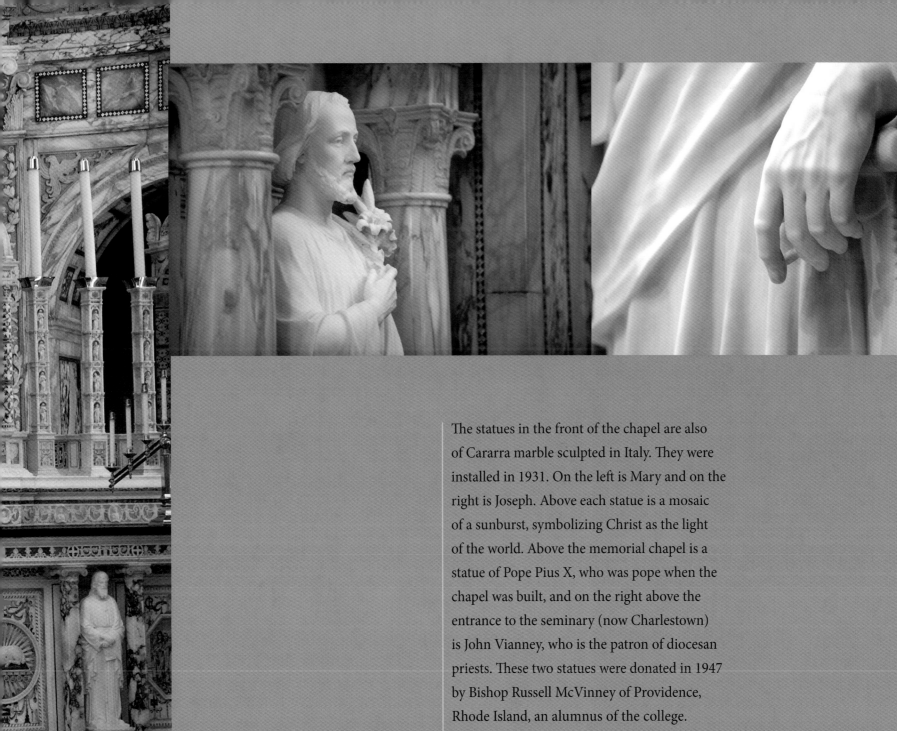

The statues in the front of the chapel are also of Cararra marble sculpted in Italy. They were installed in 1931. On the left is Mary and on the right is Joseph. Above each statue is a mosaic of a sunburst, symbolizing Christ as the light of the world. Above the memorial chapel is a statue of Pope Pius X, who was pope when the chapel was built, and on the right above the entrance to the seminary (now Charlestown) is John Vianney, who is the patron of diocesan priests. These two statues were donated in 1947 by Bishop Russell McVinney of Providence, Rhode Island, an alumnus of the college.

The organ was installed in 1919–1920, and is a Casavant pipe organ built in St. Hyacinth, Quebec. It was nicknamed the "Queen of the South" by the company, since it was the first Casavant organ to be installed in the southern United States. The organ is composed of thirty-five stops and thirty-eight ranks of pipes controlled by a three-manual console. One of the Casavant brothers who worked on the organ had previously worked for the Cavaille-Coll organ company in France, which built the great organ of St. Sulpice in Paris. Like the St. Sulpice organ, the chapel organ is particularly suited to French Romantic music. As noted earlier, St. Sulpice is the parish where the Sulpicians were founded in 1641 and is the largest church in Paris after Notre Dame. The organ was blessed by Fr. Edward Dyer, S.S., the Sulpician Superior, and a dedicatory recital was performed by Gaston Dethier on February 12, 1920.

The "Queen of the South"—the Casavant pipe organ at Our Lady of the Angels Chapel

The mosaics in the front of the chapel were fashioned by Bancel La Farge, son of American artist John La Farge. They are marvels of gold, colored glass, and tile. High above the main altar is Our Lady of the Angels, and beneath her feet in Latin are the words "Hail Queen of heaven, hail Lady of the Angels, hail root, hail gate from which came the Light of the world." The circular mosaics above and around Mary represent the instruments of the Lord's passion, beginning on the bottom right with the whip, pillar, and palm branch of the scourging; and ending on the left with the sponge, spear, and the sign on the cross naming Jesus as King of the Jews. The crown of thorns, the hammer and nails, and the chalice of suffering are also represented. The mosaic across the ceiling of the sanctuary is the Crucifixion, with the Latin words meaning "through the cross, to the light." In the center Christ is supported on the cross by God the Father and the Holy Spirit. This mosaic is signed by Bancel La Farge on the lower right. Beneath are six mosaics of angels dancing and playing various musical instruments, also by La Farge. La Farge's other works from this time include mosaics in the crypt church of the National Shrine of the Immaculate Conception in Washington, D.C. The marble mosaics on the sanctuary floor were fashioned in Italy, and the work as a whole is as fine as one could find anywhere in the world. The center mosaic under the altar is a combination of the coat of arms of Charles Carroll and that of the Sulpician Fathers. This is surrounded by the lion, the boat, the anchor, and the fish, all ancient Christian symbols. In front is a beautiful pair of peacocks, which have long been a symbol of the Resurrection. All of these mosaics were installed in the early 1920s.

The windows in the chapel were designed by one of the premier stained-glass artisans of the time, Charles Jay Connick of Boston. Connick created windows for many great worship spaces, including St. Patrick's Cathedral in New York, and University Chapel in Princeton, New Jersey. The windows for Our Lady of the Angels were among his last works. Connick supervised the construction of all the windows of the chapel except in the seven small chapels behind the altar, which were completed by his associates after his death in 1945. All of the windows designed by Connick himself were installed in time for the 1948 centennial celebration of the opening of St. Charles College in Ellicott City.

The entire group of windows is designed to celebrate in color and light, profound Christian virtues, especially as they relate to Sulpician devotion and priestly ordination.
    —Charles Jay Connick

St. Cyril and Methodius—Apostles to the Slavic Nations (detail in rose window above the organ)

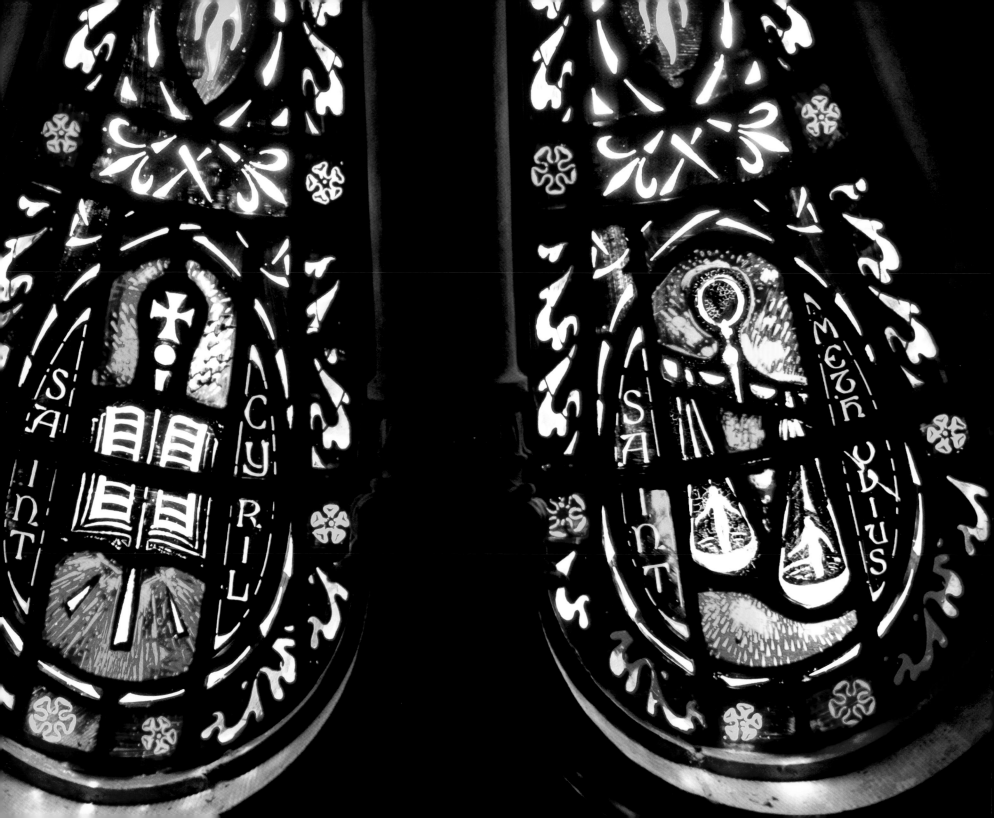

The windows in the chapel tell of the journey of the life of the priest. The aisle windows emphasize the steps in the life of a priest, beginning with the aspirant and the tonsured cleric; the minor orders of porter, lector, exorcist, and acolyte; and the major orders of subdeacon, deacon, priest, and bishop. The clerical figures on the right are complemented on the left by significant figures of the Old Testament, to celebrate the Old Testament roots of the Christian priesthood. For example, in the window with the porter, the young man holds a key to open the church, while beside him is Solomon holding the gate of the temple. Saints who serve as models to the priest—such as St. John Vianney and St. Vincent DePaul—are found in the nave windows above.

In the sanctuary are two windows flanking the altar; their closeness to the altar reflects the closeness of these figures to Christ. On the left are depicted John the Evangelist and Mary holding the child, Jesus, positioned respectively over images of the Crucifixion and of the Annunciation. The window on the right of the sanctuary contains images of Joseph and John the Baptist, which reside respectively over scenes of the nativity of Christ and the baptism of Jesus.

SOLOMO

THIS IS THE GENERATION OF THEM THAT SEEK THE LORD

THE LORD IS THE PORTION OF MY INHERITANCE

The Sacrament of Marriage (window detail in the apse chapels behind the altar)

The three rose windows represent aspects of devotion to Mary. The window above the organ is dedicated to Our Lady of the Apostles. The central figure is surrounded by petals containing symbols of apostles sent to convert the peoples of Europe—such as St. Patrick, who was sent to convert the Irish, and Sts. Cyril and Methodius, who were sent to convert the Slovaks. The window above the memorial chapel is dedicated to Our Lady of the Martyrs and commemorates the Sulpicians who were martyred during the French Revolution. Lastly, the rose window over the entrance to the seminary is dedicated to Our Lady Seat of Wisdom. The petals surrounding this central figure represent the ancient Doctors of the Church, including St. Augustine in the West and St. John Chrysostom in the East.

Below the rose window, over the entrance to the seminary, are two bay windows that represent the history of the Sulpicians and of their beginnings in the Baltimore area. In the first window are Jean Jacques Olier, who founded the Sulpicians in 1641, and Jacques Andre Emery, the Superior of the Sulpicians, who guided them through the French Revolution and arranged with Bishop Carroll for the order to come to Baltimore. In the second window are Charles Francois Nagot, who founded St. Mary's Seminary, and Oliver Jenkins, the first president of St. Charles College. Nagot is depicted holding in his hands the original building for St. Mary's Seminary—the One Mile Tavern on Paca Street in Baltimore.

The theme of the windows in the memorial chapel above the crypt in which the Jenkinses are buried is the Resurrection. On the left are figures of Christ at the tomb of Lazarus and the risen Lazarus. On the opposite side are the figures of Mary Magdalene kneeling at the tomb of Jesus and the Risen Christ.

Over all of these scenes is the dome in which the nine choirs of angels are depicted. In the center window facing the front of the chapel are Angels and Archangels. The seven remaining windows are the seven remaining choirs of angels—Dominions, Virtues, Princedoms, Powers, Seraphim, Cherubim, and Thrones.

The windows in the seven apse chapels behind the altar depict the seven sacraments. These windows were the last to be installed in the chapel, and their completion inspired one priest to observe that "these windows have turned the chapel into a veritable jewel-box, a symphony in light and color…As long as St. Charles shall endure, its chapel will remain the center of its work."

Windows in the chapel dome, depicting two of the nine choirs of angels

Window details from the apse chapels behind the altar. From left to right: the Chapel of the Last Annointing, the Holy Spirit Window, and the Chapel of the Eucharist.

The Stations of the Cross are fourteen small mosaics on the walls of the chapel, which represent fourteen moments in the journey of Christ from His condemnation by Pilate to His being laid in the tomb. These mosaics were fashioned in Italy and installed in the chapel in 1964. In the memorial chapel is another mosaic installed in 1964 by the Rambusch Company of New York, depicting Jesus coming forth from the tomb. This company also designed and installed the eight brass chandeliers in the front of the chapel.

Although other projects for the chapel,
including additional statues and mosaics,
were envisioned by the donors, major work
on the interior of the chapel was essentially
completed with the installation of the
mosaics in 1964. The chapel continued to
be the spiritual home to many hundreds of
seminarians until the seminary closed in 1977
due to declining enrollment. The last Mass
celebrated for the seminary community was
the graduation ceremony in May 1977, and
it was presided over by Cardinal Lawrence
Sheehan, 12th Archbishop of Baltimore
and an alumnus of St. Charles College. The
graduation address was given by renowned
church historian The Reverend John Tracy
Ellis, who spoke of the long and distinguished
history of St. Charles College and of its great
contributions to the American Church.

Easter Vigil Mass, 2008

After the closing of the college, despite being used by several groups including the Lamb of God School, the chapel fell into general disrepair. It was in 1983 that the chapel was rescued and a new phase of its life was begun. In that year the seminary property was purchased from the Sulpicians by John Erickson and returned to the Lord's service with the development of Charlestown Retirement Community. The name Charlestown symbolized continuity with the history of the property. In 2008 Charlestown celebrated its 25th anniversary. Although the chapel and the Sulpician cemetery remained under the ownership of the Sulpicians and St. Mary's Seminary in Baltimore, the chapel was destined to play a prominent role in the life of Charlestown. John Erickson and the Sulpicians initiated much-needed repairs to the chapel so that it could be used by the residents of Charlestown.

Recital by Virginia Reinecke at Our Lady of the Angels, February 2008

Our Lady of the Angels Chapel became and remains the religious and cultural center of life at Charlestown. It is home to two religious congregations: Our Lady of the Angels Parish of the Catholic Archdiocese of Baltimore, and Charlestown United Protestant Church. In a *Baltimore Sun* article dated December 26, 1994, The Reverend Warren West, pastor of the Protestant church, said this of the chapel: "It is very conducive to worship, it is packed every Sunday. The organ is magnificent, the acoustics and aesthetics are wonderful. It is the most beautiful worship center in the Baltimore area." Both congregations have full religious services for residents, and together, the staffs serve as the Pastoral Care Department of Charlestown. Other religious services as well as ecumenical programs, weddings, and, of course, funerals are regularly held in the chapel. The chapel is also home to two concert series: the Chapel Concert Series operated by Charlestown residents, and the Our Lady of the Angels Concert Series operated by the Catholic parish. The official Charlestown logo, the sunburst, was adapted from the mosaics above the statues of Mary and Joseph in the front of the chapel. Although Reverend West was certainly correct concerning the beauty of the chapel and the wonderful sound of the organ, by the mid 1990s it was obvious that the organ and the chapel were still in dire need of a great deal of work. In 1995 the campaign for the restoration of **Our Lady of the Angels Chapel** was launched, and work was scheduled to begin the following year.

In the *Baltimore Sun* edition of March 2, 1996, there appeared an article about the restoration of the Casavant organ that was installed in 1919. The article stated that "the queen of the South had succumbed to age and was desperately in need of repair." The organ had had a new console installed in 1969, but the entire instrument was badly in need of repair and upgrading. Brides could not have the Trumpet Voluntary in C played at their wedding because the pipes for the entire key of C were not in working order. The 1996 renovation included the repair or replacement of these pipes and the addition of eight new ranks of pipes as well as the removal of two ranks that were no longer needed. New windchests and reservoirs, which regulate the flow of air to the pipes, were also built. These and the new pipes were fashioned in the Casavant workshop in St. Hyacinth, Quebec. The upstairs console was rebuilt and a computer memory was installed. A second console was also added downstairs in the sanctuary. A dedicatory recital was performed on September 14, 1997, by Daniel Roth, Titular Organist of the Church of St. Sulpice in Paris.

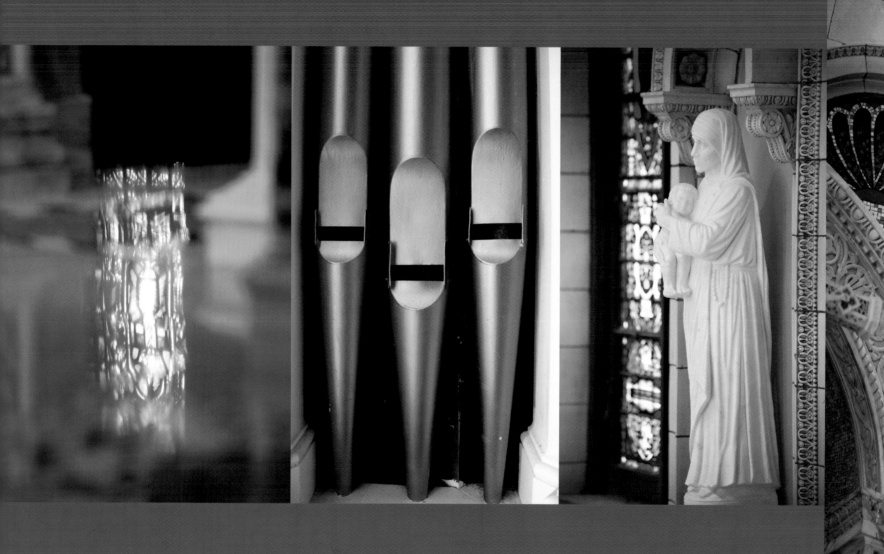

TOP, CENTER: *Casavant organ pipes*

TOP, RIGHT: *Statue of Mother Teresa of Calcutta*

RIGHT: *Mosaics above the altar*

With the renovation of the organ there began a ten-year process of much-needed restoration and repair as well as completion of considerable work in the chapel originally intended but never accomplished. Much of this work was generously funded by residents of Charlestown, St. Mary's Seminary, alumni of the seminary, and John and Nancy Erickson. Both religious congregations also made generous contributions. After the restoration of the organ was accomplished, the next priority was a new lighting system. The chapel had never really had an adequate lighting system, and much of its artistic beauty could not even be seen. The lighting system dated to the 1950s. A new system was designed and installed by the firm of Spears/ Votta and Associates of Baltimore. The new system bathed the entire chapel in light as never before and revealed the full beauty of the many artistic treasures. The cold cathode lighting in the front arches and the dome is what accomplished this and was the only known example of its kind in the nation at the time of installation. The firm was recognized for the excellence of their work in the chapel with an award from the Illuminating Engineering Society of North America.

Much of the repair work during this period was accomplished by Santo Navarria, a local tile and mosaic master artist. His family was from Italy and had been in this work for five generations. He began by restoring the intricate Italian mosaic work on the sanctuary floor, which had been heavily damaged over the years. The marble and tiles necessary for the restoration had to be imported from Italy, and the work took three years to complete. This restoration and the new lighting system were funded by a generous gift from the Carl Holzaphel family of Baltimore. This was the largest gift to the chapel since the original gift by the Jenkinses. Over the course of ten years, Mr. Navarria also cleaned and polished the Carrara marble that completely lined the walls of the chapel. The new lighting system had made it obvious just how much dirt had accumulated on the marble since it was installed in the 1920s.

During this period of restoration, several projects for the chapel that were originally planned but never completed were also brought to life. It was the residents of Charlestown who pointed out that these projects should be completed as originally envisioned. In the front of the chapel on the walls of the two transepts, beneath the rose windows were sixteen spaces where mosaics of some kind were intended. These spaces had always been empty, and no record of the original intent for their decoration could be found. Given the name of the chapel and the presence of so many angels, it seemed that angels of some kind would be appropriate for the spaces, and so Santo Navarria designed and fabricated a mosaic choir of angels holding their choir books to complement the angels behind the marble altar holding their musical instruments. To reflect an international flavor, the angels represent various races and nationalities. All the material for the mosaics was imported from Italy, and the work was funded by residents of Charlestown as memorials to their loved ones.

Also on the walls of the nave of the chapel, between the windows, there were eight empty pedestals that were intended for statues of the saints. Marble statues for these pedestals, as well as for the backs of the two lower side aisles, were ordered from Italy. They are made of the same Carrara marble as the rest of the statues in the chapel. The statues were originally planned to be of male saints who could be models for the seminarians. However, since the chapel was already filled with male imagery (as it was a seminary chapel), it was decided that the new statues would be of women, a fitting tribute to the many female residents of Charlestown. As with the angel mosaics, these statues were funded as memorials by residents of Charlestown. The statues include Mother Teresa of Calcutta holding a baby (a clue that the statues are not original to the chapel but are recent additions) and Margaret Mary Alacoque, a seventeenth-century French nun who received the vision of the Sacred Heart and helped to spread the Devotion to the Sacred Heart throughout France and from there to the whole world.

TOP, CENTER: *St. John Vianney*

FACING PAGE: *St. Therese of Lisieux*

Four of the statues are of Americans: Kateri Tekakwitha, a Mohawk Native American from upstate New York who became a Catholic in the seventeenth century; Mother Elizabeth Ann Seton, who founded the Daughters of Charity in the United States and started the first Catholic elementary school in the country at St. Mary's Seminary in Baltimore; Mother Mary Lange, who founded the first Catholic order of African American women in the world in 1829 in Baltimore; and Mother Frances Xavier Cabrini, who came from Italy in the late 1800s to work with Italian immigrants. Mother Cabrini herself became an American citizen, and in 1946 she became the first American citizen to be canonized a saint. Both Mother Seton and Mother Lange professed their vows and founded their communities in the chapel of St. Mary's Seminary. Also represented are the three women named Doctors of the Church: Teresa of Avila, Catherine of Siena, and, in the lower aisle, Therese of Lisieux.

In the memorial chapel are two statues that were gifts to the chapel from residents of Charlestown in the year 2000. On the left is a sixteenth century Spanish wood carving of the Risen Christ, which appears to have at one time been

"The Americans"—statues of American saints at Our Lady of the Angels

damaged by fire. It was acquired by the previous owner, who was in the Diplomatic Corp, when he was stationed in South America. On the right is a magnificent fifteenth century statue of the Virgin of the Apocalypse carved from one block of limewood. The statue is from Germany and is said to have come from the workshop and school of Tillmann Riemenschneider (1460–1531), the leading German sculptor and wood carver of that time. The characteristic features of his style are certainly present in this statue, and a very similar statue by Riemenschneider is in the medieval collection of the Metropolitan Museum of Art in New York. This statue was acquired by the previous owner in Germany at the end of World War II—the church from which it came having been destroyed. These statues are the only works of art in the chapel from Spain and Germany. The latest addition, in 2007, is a statue behind the main altar in one of the chapels of the seven sacraments of the Sedes Sapientiae (Seat of Wisdom)—the Patroness of the Sulpicians. The statue was sculpted in Italy and was donated by a resident in memory of her husband. It holds special meaning in the chapel: in the days of the seminary, a copy of this statue of Mary was in every classroom and student room in the college.

Fifteenth century German statue of the Virgin of the Apocalypse

Our Lady of the Angels overlooking Baltimore and the Maryland countryside

On January 14, 2008, the Most Reverend Edwin O'Brien made his first visit to Our Lady of the Angels Chapel. O'Brien is the 15th Archbishop of Baltimore and the successor of both Archbishop Carroll, who brought the Sulpicians to this country, and Cardinal Gibbons, who laid the cornerstone of the chapel. On entering the chapel, the archbishop simply stood and tried to take it all in. He then said, "I've heard a lot about this place, but you really have to see it to believe it." He was so right. You will never really believe it until you see it. St. Charles has endured, and Our Lady of the Angels Chapel remains the center of its life.

This is, so far, the story of Our Lady of the Angels Chapel in words and pictures. It is a place of incomparable beauty and spiritual depth, home to thousands of seminarians throughout the years and now to the residents of Charlestown. May it always stand as it has, to the honor and glory of Almighty God and to the service of His holy people.

Larrivee is a Priest of the Society
ce, and he attended St. Charles
rom 1969 to 1973. For the
years Father Leo has been the
ur Lady of the Angels Parish at
vn.

Jim Stratton lives near Baltimore, Maryland,
and works as an engineer in the aerospace
industry. Jim specializes in fine art and
wedding photography, and his images have
appeared in several online magazines and
travel guides. *Our Lady of the Angels* is
Jim's first full-length book. Selected images
from his portfolio can be viewed at
www.jimstrattonphotography.com.